D1308625

Rounding the Human Corners

Rounding the Human Corners

POEMS

Linda Hogan

Introduction by William Kittredge

COFFEE HOUSE PRESS

MINNEAPOLIS

2008

COFFEE HOUSE PRESS books are available to the trade through our primary distributor, Consortium Book Sales & Distribution, www.cbsd.com or (800) 283-3572. For personal orders, catalogs, or other information, write to: Coffee House Press, 27 North Fourth Street, Suite 400, Minneapolis, MN 55401.

Coffee House Press is a nonprofit literary publishing house. Support from private foundations, corporate giving programs, government programs, and generous individuals helps make the publication of our books possible. We gratefully acknowledge their support in detail in the back of this book.

To you and our many readers around the world, we send our thanks
for your continuing support.

LIBRARY OF CONGRESS CIP INFORMATION
Library of Congress Cataloging-in-Publication Data
Hogan, Linda.
Rounding the human corners / Linda Hogan.
p. cm.
ISBN-13: 978-1-56689-210-0 (alk. paper)
ISBN-10: 1-56689-206-6
I. Title.
PS3558.034726R68 2008
811'.54—DC22
2007046388

FIRST EDITION | FIRST PRINTING

1 3 5 7 9 8 6 4 2

PRINTED IN THE U.S.A.

ACKNOWLEDGMENTS

The author is grateful to the following magazines and books for the previous acceptance of poems appearing in this book: *Parabola: A Magazine of Tradition and Myth, American Poetry Review, Shenandoah, Spirituality and Health, Agenda: US Edition, Dry Creek Review, Light: Studies in American Indian Literature, Wilderness Magazine, Nimrod, New Letters, National Millennium Survey, Pembroke, Bare Root, Image,* and others.

Thanks to the following for their support for me and this work: with love to Margo Solod, Deborah Miranda, Peggy Shumaker, Allison Hedge-Coke. You have helped me survive part of a year. Thanks also to David Curtis, Kathleen Cain, Marilyn Auer, Cathy Stanton, and Lisa Wagner. You have been good friends to me.

For this forgiving land.
And toward a growing human wisdom.

Contents

AFFINITY

The Way Nature Behaves

William Kittredge

Linda Hogan is a poet who will lead you to think about, as Rilke said, changing your life, which will help you back off and re-imagine sensible and spontaneous ways to move through the hours and days. As a child we instinctively understood the processes of playing and wondering and cherishing. When did we lose track? Poets like Linda, through their language, open for us a doorway into their specific resonating dream of the electric universe.

But Linda Hogan, one of those singular poets, doesn't much resort to that kind of abstract language. She talks of things she sees and touches and tastes and of odors, things she both fears and cherishes—what we might call "the actual," as in her poem "Alone."

What if, for a man lost
in the wide, cold reach of sea,
no boat glides toward him, no rope is thrown,
or the woman with beautiful hands doesn't miss him?

Even so it would be beautiful, the blue, the white
floating immensity.

The actual—that impossibly complex metaphor where we are, at sea in ourselves, terrified and reminded that we could also calm down and enjoy some last few chances at rapture as it is said some do when sure they are perishing. She talks of cougars and horses, mustang mares.

In "The Night Constant"

At night, outside the house,
I feel the lion

she goes on

I feel it with the naked eye of skin,
the fine hair, the animal trappings of my body

and she laments

and with all the lies we tell ourselves
so we won't see the world collapse
but when it does
it is not from what is known
but from what is never seen.

In "The Horses," she writes

there is no freedom here, not any more

and

do you remember
the forgotten language wild,
can you still call it?

But cougars and horses are powerful and proud "charismatic mega fauna" and commonly glorified. Linda is equally persuasive when contemplating relationships with the billions of tiny creatures which swarm the earth. In "Moving the Woodpile," she begins

Never am I careless
yet when I lift the wood,

A mistake: she has destroyed *the beautiful work of insects*, and thinks of them as *following the light even when it is cruel*. What's destroyed is a wasp's nest.

How everything small and nearly gone
is precious, the paper wasp nest,
made by the moment by moment creation of care

XII

She speaks of mud daubers and blue dragonflies and a perfect circle of humming gnats.

> I've always wished
> to hold the truly stolen, broken world together
> but my every move is to break
> by degrees, acres, even the smallest atom.

Solace comes through apprehending the material and holy world precisely as it is. These are the last words in "Deer Dance."

> their gray brown bodies
> the scars of fences
> the fur never quite straight
> as if they'd just stepped into it.

Here, we're in touch with an instant in an evolving process we can only experience in flashes and comprehend as a miracle that keeps on. It's where we are. Linda helps us see freshly, blinders off.

Recently I learned that Linda has been given, among many honors, the Spirit of the West Literary Achievement Award by the Mountains and Plains Independent Booksellers. Her poems deserve all possible congratulation. They are so very amply useful as they take us back to the essence of what and where we are.

Eucalyptus

It is the first red light of morning
and the others are praying outside with old songs,
sage and tobacco, while I have been dreaming
from the deep, the ancient,
taking in the red light rising
between the eucalyptus trees
and their fragrance.
They dropped three seeds in the shadows,
three deep shrines,
worlds becoming, I can hold them.
And the naked bark,
its spare intimacy
that peels back and reveals its other layers
deeper, earlier.
Without effort, that beautiful undoing,
the smooth newness.

Some of the religious say the five senses are thieves
so let's say I am stolen
because my senses are all awake
and like the tree I can lose myself
layer after layer
all the way down to infinity
and that's when the world has eyes and sees.
The whole world
loves the unlayered human.

Unlayering the Human

The Way In

Sometimes the way to milk and honey is through the body.
Sometimes the way in is a song.
But there are three ways in the world: dangerous, wounding,
and beauty.
To enter stone, be water.
To rise through hard earth, be plant
desiring sunlight, believing in water.
To enter fire, be dry.
To enter life, be food.

Journey

The mouth of the river may be beautiful.
It doesn't remember the womb of its beginning.
It doesn't look back to where it's been
or wonder who ahead of it polished the rough stones.

It is following the way
in its fullness,
now like satin,
now cresting,
waters meeting, kindred
to travel gathered together,
all knowing it flows
one way, shining or in shadows.
And me, the animal
I ride wants to drive forward,
its longing not always my own,
overrunning its banks and bounds,
edgeless, spilling along the way

because, as I forget,
it knows everything
is before it.

Inside

How something is made flesh
no one can say. The buffalo soup
becomes a woman
who sings every day to her horses
or summons another to her private body
saying come, touch, this is how
it begins, the path of a newly born
who, salvaged from other lives and worlds,
will grow to become a woman, a man,
with a heart that never rests,
and the gathered berries,
the wild grapes
enter the body,
human wine
which can love,
where nothing created is wasted;
the swallowed grain
takes you though the dreams
of another night,
the deer meat becomes hands
strong enough to work.

But I love most
the white-haired creature
eating green leaves;

the sun shines there
swallowed, showing in her face
taking in all the light,

and in the end
when the shadow from the ground
enters the body and remains,
in the end, you might say,
This is myself
still unknown, still a mystery.

Humble

Where the road ends,
where the land ends,
where layers of earth history
are revealed by the constant taking
of the sea,
a solitary house stands in ocean spray.
Once filled with life, no one lives here.
All is abandoned, yet it still makes a stand
in the place where the people of the whale lived.
You'd think whatever forces there are
would at least have taken this into their arms,
embraced in love,
but even stars come apart
in the play of universal wind.
I love this house of unrest,
the handiwork ever to be outdone
by the carpenter of wind,
the craftsman of waves.
As for me, loving the lone house
perhaps because it is so like the body,
that other amazing architecture waiting,
also believing the world should open its arms
and hold it in a great kindness,
not merely to be salt and skin, dissolving
day by day.

I am still a beginner in this world
without a hold, without money or love or tools.
I am down on my knees.
Maybe now I can begin to learn something.

The Given

Some say our lives come from the wind.
The human, others say, is made by the mother of corn,
or clay given breath, a rib,
or comes from the great dreaming,
a congress of words and songs.

We walked out of the ocean, barely,
and gave ourselves to earth
and the ancients gave us our secret names
knowing, being human, we would forget them.

And yes, there was the one who carried a pitcher
full with the nectar of immortality
given only to the gods.
And the Chinese said there were 365 gods of the body
but to speak their names was to lose them.

I think of this, watching those who are walking today
into the river in garments of white, offering themselves,
their names, to save their souls.

Every day I ask myself, what is a human?
The present is so bare and tender
like the garments of the newly saved
I can see through, the revealed

nipples, thighs, buttocks
and I wonder which of the 365 gods
are inside the body today
and if in the future
when the air leaves your lungs
and, as some say, you stand at the beginning
of a tunnel,
you remember your name.
No, not that one, the real one,
The Given, the one
lost somewhere
along the way.

Gentling the Human

There are five holy places in the body:
the heart, the spirit, the secret, the mysterious,
and the deeply hidden.

These are the ones with the power
of gentling the human.

And the human is clouds,
lung, mist, and heart,
a pulse at the wrist,
and the spirit
which belongs to the mountain,
and since it's said we come
from the east
where first life might pass
over a lake one day
or drift toward the ocean like the wind
it came from,
or follow a slant of snow,
and then there may be one of these,
a place
where the spirit sets down.

It's said, too, that we come from the wind,
born from it, yet we are given flesh

and bone, the milk teeth which fall
when a child passes through.

A human is breath,
current and tide,
yet merely
a woman of light,
a man of fire,
the bare skin so vulnerable,
fragrant and leaf-blessed as we are.

Here she comes, walking.
Here he is, as if
undressed from the body,
as if the abyss were beautiful
and nothing there could hold you down.

This is the time when the spirit has no need for teeth
and in the time it takes pollen to light
the wild world tames us.
Oh, it is so soft and full, the human now,
and suddenly you are in the clearing.
To the east is the mountain
with sweet, sweet rain.

Mysteries of the Bed

Darkness.
When moths fly away from the blown-out light,
the bed is an island.

Among cottons and rumpled cloths
is unquestioned passion,
a memory of the future,
and the newly born and purely clean
is given to the mother.

Between the human and all the rest
lies only an eyelid.
Asleep, a person is unburdened,
the human no longer a hunter.
A cat climbs to the chest
and sits with the rise and fall of breath.
A child cries himself to sleep,
a woman turns inward,
or a man toward perfume.

The bed holds a person from before history
and the many claims of darkness,
though nothing here is owned.
The greeds that lie
within ourselves give way.

In the house of flesh,
the vines of what is daily unremembered
climb walls and enter doors,
reach across closed windows,
seed themselves in the cracked roof.
Above, storms pass over.
There are galaxies. The turn of stars,
and directions no one follows by day
are taken. You go there, fearless for once,
to where we slept on moss in the forest
with planets in a known circle
of sky above, to where there was never a roof,
and there is bone memory,
the opening of other eyes,
to vision with no seeing.
Even in the coldest heart,
we are mostly tender here,
swimmers breathing.
You are suddenly in still, clean water.
The rocks at the bottom of the pool
are clear.

It does all this because there is something
just as close to grace as death
and just as close to mercy
and because something in a life
has to matter.

The Shepherd's Cabin

Walking yesterday
I stopped by the shepherd's cabin once again.
I apologize to the air, forgive me,
because I always look inside
though nothing ever changes.
The sugar bowl is on the table, perfect.
The clothing has flowers never faded,
and the house seems full,
or it rains and I hear it on the tin roof
and think of my own childhood.
I see him lifting the cup,
sitting in silence,
his house so tidy
but all summer he wanders.
Then I wake up one morning
and hear the bell around the goat's neck,
and the hooves of the horse,
and the talking of sheep,
and I know the grasses will be gone.
Or sometimes he rides the horse to the door
and hands me a package of cookies,
the dog down on its haunches moving sheep.
Maybe I go to hold the lamb
and pet the dog or horse and all are fresh
from the pines, the hanging moss,

the green floor of the world that so
makes us want to live.
I think he is happy
like a far traveler
of the soul who can't quite return
to the body or eyes, all those.
I only hear the bell and know at his place
is solitude. Beautiful. Chosen.
The pilot light still burning.

Rapture

Who knows the mysteries of the poppies
when you look across the red fields,
or hear the sound of long thunder,
then the saving rain.
Everything beautiful,
the solitude of the single body
or sometimes, too, when the body is kissed
on the lips or hands or eyelids tender.
Oh for the pleasure of living in a body.
It may be, it may one day be
this is a world haunted by happiness,
where people finally are loved
in the light of leaves,
the feel of bird wings passing by.
Here it might be that no one wants power.
They don't want more.
And so they are in the forest,
old trees,
or those small but grand.
And when you sleep, rapture, beauty,
may seek you out.
Listen. There is
secret joy,
sweet dreams you may never forget.
How worthy the being

in the human body. If,
when you are there, you see women
wading on the water
and clouds in the valley,
the smell of rain,
or a lotus blossom rises out of round green leaves,
remember there is always something
besides our own misery.

The Small

The world, too, gives up
its small, life-bearing and insensible
losses to light, the least,
though beautiful in its decay,
the deer by the creek
with the shining beetles
crawling through its innards,
the desperate pollens
in glorious shapes and armor
in the swells of a visible breeze,
night's fungus and foxfire
grown on the collapse of plants
shines as if to welcome the humble rising
the luminous falling
of the world.
Here the foundation,
rare elements, robust nitrogen,
the least, all bright,
all the way down
to the wayward human body
itself falling through time lightly,
the spinal fluid
made of shining crystals.
Who would have guessed
everything as it disappears,
burning with new life,
the dead at last,
all, finally, enlightened.

Awake

Waking today
just before winter
when I try to name the color of grasses,
how I feel their beauty,
there is no word.
I think of the time before there were words,
when you would know morning mist by the feel
of your loved one's skin and hair,
and when someone came from the forest of dry leaves
you would know them by their scent
even if they carried no wood.
Or the heat of their body skin in summer.
Or if they came the winding way
down from the mountains
they would be covered in cloud
returning to the fold,
or if they had gone farther, to the ocean,
you'd know them by their far-seeing eyes,
and when some travelers return
and are shining with light
you know, without saying, that they have been
in touch with other worlds.
I have no wealth to speak of
other than this,
all this, just to praise the dry grasses
and their color that can't be spoken in words.

Light

In the first morning of the world created,
on the skin of water reflected,
is the spread of a sun,
and the sun, like god, is a power
you cannot see,
only what it lights on,
only what it touches with warmth,
and yet it always has a shadow at its feet.

Then there is the sea, the sheer weight of it,
the lightness of its creatures,
some silver
as they leap above it,
and those at the bottom
making their own light
in what would have been
night infinite, as if the sea carries no
shadows at its feet.

Then there is the light of wood decaying
out by the stagnant pond,
where the eyes of prey nearby
shine in the dark, betrayed

as when the deer stares one last time
to see if the hunter still follows
out in the shadows of living trees.

One man I knew fished the sea
and told me of silver fishes falling
from the mouth of a netted one.
Perhaps in the last breath
we give back all the swallowed,
all the taken-in, and it is light, after all,
first and last, we live for, die for.
We fly toward it
like those who return from it say.

But for now, for here, we fly without will
toward it, drink a glass of it,
see it through green leaves, love it.
There, walk toward it.
Lift it, it has no weight.
Carry it, breathe it, cherish it.

You want to know why god is far away
and we are only shadows at his feet?
Tell me, how long does it take a moth
to reach the moon?

Spring

There is a place in the ocean where fresh water enters,
where a spring so small comes from beneath,
different water no one sees,
yet freshwater shrimp and tubeworms
will find this hidden water
from the underworld,
beings who dwell
in the surrounds of infinity.

Swimming, I feel its touch on my legs
where it wells up from under the great weight
of an ocean, fresh, the warm feel of love
against skin, as if something new could come from it.

There is a line between sweetness and salt.
This water, if you could find it,
you could drink it.
You could contain it
before it is taken in by something greater.

In Time

I have my mother's wrist,
my father's hands.
I walk on the same ankle bones
of a three-million-year-old amphibian.
In such a world is the nature
of limbs, the floating rib,
the creation of bone
grown long from infancy
and nerve following pathways known
to the future
from the past when God's arm, once wing,
once fin,
swam through an ocean of creation
and reached out
to climb the shores of a world
without a knowing care for what we would become,
our evolved hand,
sinew giving way for monsters and kings
for prayer and the trigger finger
becoming stronger,
the human muscle,
and all this from a single cell.
Oh the beautiful water-filled
of our kind
and the gods of creation

waiting for beginnings.
We are their love, their misery
awaiting the new
betrayal, betrayer of the elegant, tender bones.

We Will Feed You

In the morning, I hear the chants
of the paddlers, the canoe nations
on their sea journey coming in with the tide
over a forest of seaweed.
There is a story in the large single tree
that carries them on water.
The story is long.
They sing it and tell it their names.

First, I saw them
as if they rose from the sea
one after the other
same as the waves
and I ran to meet them
the paddlers of the black canoes
as if they were my tribe
when we came to this land
from the other side of America
meeting de Soto, becoming slaves.

Then at night the dancers,
the heart of the singers
come into my heart,
the blankets with salmon
and buttons as if closing and opening

the history on their backs.
All were there: eagle, whale, frog, raven,
the world.

There are times I long
for the beginning,
that canoe of my own people
seeing the flowers
so beautiful, and the birds of all colors
as we journey,
myself a cell of someone's body,
seeing it through their eyes,
but this time I only wish to be on this coast
sleeping with the old ones
in a village newly revealed
up from the ocean,
this edge of being there,
the cedar of the canoes
of the beautiful,
and light in morning
the man saying,
We will feed you.
We will care for you.
You may step upon our land.

Rounding the Human Corners

Loneliness

They say there are only four chambers of the heart.
I know there are five
and that fifth one opened,
not opened, but broke.
It was a pure thing, that moment.

And if my heart could kneel down
and if my spirit could call back that moment,
if my body hadn't begun its ripening
into old age
and been also as young as the first grape in an arbor
believing in future wine, it wouldn't.

Loneliness had to prove again
that I was only human
and there was one part of myself not yet
given.

And hearing the gnats that day in their circle above us,
the smell of earth around us,
the wild grass, altogether so natural
as if I was, we were, alive with it,
as if I was not a human separate, but earth,
part of it again,

as splendid as the deer standing in trees
or the blue dragonflies in air.

I longed to be a flowering branch,
the sea in its rocking, an unguessed world.

Even now it seems so much as if the body was only
the desire of the planet,
as if it could turn itself into the universe
both together, the same,
because such a thing is irrational flesh,
irrational earth.

Sounding the Depths

I think sometimes of entering the water,
silently diving to the world beneath,
to the dark quiet of deep water.
I don't know water; I've never seen
the fish with light,
never wished to uncover a mystery
to be the first to sound any depths
to say Am I not wonderful
for this journey,
this courage.

It's just that the place calls to me
from inside,
elemental yearning for element

The pull of all water toward the ocean,
the hope that somewhere
there is a world undisturbed,
that when we enter, it closes behind us
as if we never were here.
Someplace a source,
a place without despair,
the beginning.

And the distance, I know
from here to there is great.

The Heron

I am always watching
the single heron at its place
alone at water, its open eye,
one leg lifted
or wading without seeming to move.

It is a mystery seen
but never touched
until this morning
when I lift it from its side
where it lays breathing.
I know the beak that could attack,
that unwavering golden eye
seeing me, my own saying I am harmless,
but if I had that eye, nothing would be safe.
The claws hold tight my hand,
its dun-brown feathers, and the gray
so perfectly laid down.

The bird is more beautiful
than my hand, skin more graceful
than my foot, my own dark eye
so much more vulnerable,
the heart beating quickly,
its own language speaking,

You could kill me or help me.
I know you and I have no choice
but to give myself up
and in whatever supremacy of this moment,
hold your human hand
with my bent claws.

Enigma

On which day of creation did the insects appear,
the one that looks like a leaf
with all the green veins,
the one that mimics a twig,
the mantis I picked up,
the color of my skin
as if it could hide there,
the eye-winged moth, watching,
the beetles who wrote their stories in wood
before they flew.
I wasn't at any of their births
and know I missed the fashioning of angels
who have learned to hide their great lives.

Tonight I sit by my lamp
and watch two dragonflies enter the room
with green wings.

The mystery is that I don't match their beauty,
their lace, their silken powders,
their praise of sun,
the known glory of a breeze,
but I am happy. For tonight
everything I could want is here.

There's no searching, no wanting,
and I don't know on which day of creation
such happiness was made
and signed by thin feet.

Alone

How many nautical miles do we swim to enter a world
after floating, after having been stars,
after emerging alone out of a sleeping world,
out of the contained darkness of a single human body.
At first the world is all water. The curved,
unfixed bones of the head drift
pale as a beluga I saw once beneath water.
Then, like first continents, the bones drift together
to form one land, or something nearly whole, nearly strong,
the infant beginning. It, he, she will be bathed
in the seawater, red brine, and the fallen light of planets.

Sometimes birth is violent
as the edge of a calving glacier in a world shaped by ice.
Sometimes birth is soft,
tender as the first sight of a loved one
or a green fern
pushing aside the whole weight of earth.

Sometimes death, too, is delicate
as ice floes in late spring
thinned and set afloat by sun and time and warmth,
from the place where winter is
a night of constant darkness,
and summer a midnight light.

Once I heard about a hunter
standing on ice
waiting for a seal to come up to breathe.
Waiting, lost in thought,
he found himself
adrift, floating toward the sea
with nothing to anchor or hold him.

Maybe, on his knees, waiting for the animal
to surface and breathe,
he'd been thinking of the beauty of lasting dawn
or how one morning
light fell across a woman's thin-fingered hand
beautiful from work.

What if, for a man lost
in the wide, cold reach of sea,
no boat glides toward him, no rope is thrown,
or the woman with beautiful hands doesn't miss him?

Even so it would be beautiful, the blue, the white
floating immensity.

In this place they say
the whales are children who died
and didn't want to return as humans.
That's why they smile so beautifully
moving up from dark water

to take a breath,
emerging to look at us a moment
before floating back into the unknown.
Do they remember long ago,
when they dwelt
in the dark uncharted world of human life,
recalling nights or lamps
or even the moments of human loneliness
and love, the mortal doors,
how they open and close
with love or solitude.

Thinking all this,
I sometimes wish myself to disappear
back to the birthing sea
and glide away
with the whales I have seen,
and sometimes I am silent,
feeling the marvelous wave
of something no one knows made flesh.

Anatomy

Inside the womb of the mother,
the spine is the first formed,
even before the heart begins
and all the pathways of the body soon
will lead there, the contents
of which you can never doubt,
the red rush of blood
as if we swim with fire
or it with us in a circular flood.

After birth, the navel remains
so you can never forget you weren't a first person,
but one humble from the past, soon
to disappear into the future.

We are noble gases and crude elements, carbon,
and through history have been wrapped in silk,
encased in gold,
embalmed with cloves, amber, pollen,
as we have also been torn to the bone
and treated as if not ever divine or vulnerable
by the rages and fears of others.

But what body part is it that dreams?
Not the lens of the eye, not the ear,

but an unknown part entranced,
the part that listens to gods,
speaks to mortals,
the one who, at the end,
when it all comes apart
and the soul leaves, not merely like at night
in a dream,
you think of the heart,
how love should be the last thing to disappear
with the history of a person's life bent by time,
or the ripening of bruised beauty.

Remember, then the first thing to form was the spine
but the last to disappear
is the sacrum, the tailbone,
as if the body remembers the fine animal
that was lost
some place in time.

Whale Rising

Breath. Behind us.
Milk creature, she has navigated the world
by whale map, this ancient mother,
and we see ourselves
inside the large dark eye
that takes our human measure,
history unspeakable,
and nothing to hide behind.

What moves the waves we cannot see,
nor can we know what moves a whale
to rise upward to the daughters of her enemies
except for faith in air,
and we sit in the boat for hours now,
blown by breeze and tide,
moved by the mystery that, like all mystery,
could sink or drown us.

Beneath water is the blue, infinite
light from the bottom of ocean.
No one returns from there unchanged
by everything larger, that dark eye
that fixed us in its gaze, the clouds
behind us, the wind-breath of a stormy world,

the exquisite smell of fish and krill
from inside a great life.

I want you to know they are beautiful,
the songs from beneath this world,
rising up from water
as we sit in the boat,
held in the fold of its song,
lost in the mist of its breath.

On the Small Toe

They are the most innocent
of all the body,
the toes
like the blind wasp infants
in the nest of darkness
not quite ever seeming
most alive
to bear the weight they do,
the smallest one hardly without
a hint of claw
or even finger of an ape.
You could almost believe
there is no evolution
but that we are returning
to a kind of grace
in this life. Oh god, or sky creature,
or earth, whatever of creation is there,
thank you for this one
body part that sees so fortunately little
but bears so much
hiding there in the dark.
It doesn't need to turn an eye
or ear. It is already a mystic in a cave,
in animal skin.

Little does it care for miracles.
It doesn't even want to move by itself,
old, old grandmother
preparing in time to leave the body.

The Radiant

In night,
at the dark limits of earth
where land ends and water begins,
at the elemental border
where you can go no further
without one entering the other,
the green light goes on.
It's not the man who fishes here,
not a light of human making
because we are the ones who measure light
and because light was created before us
from blood of flesh and sea
like this animal light of the manta ray
traveling the latitudes of night
and longitudes of darkness
knowing the blue unfathomable shifts
and dark ranges of the world beneath water.

It travels a rich sea away from us,
its light falling on plankton,
bringing food and fish toward it,
as if it is moonlight
opening across water,
it passes over the fished-out places
beyond the reef where coral is dying,

out past the point where the British captain was killed
by those who first thought he was a shining god.

It moves steadily out into darkness
to where the colder darkness begins to well up
from the sea depths that have no bottom,
the place where I have feared the pale face of a shark
with its deadly touch
against my naked legs.

The ray travels over the many
other lives that have light
and below them is the blindness
of fish who need no sight,
and out toward the place where sun left the sky,
to where the larger creatures live,
where fishermen once found their boat cast in shadow
and looking up, saw what kind of cloud it was,
the manta ray risen out of water, a leap
so large it darkened the sky.
The men returned haunted by
everything that was larger than they were,
more beautiful and bearing its own light.

Tonight on this dark shore,
watching the animal light go over the horizon,
I long to be in water heading for open sea,
for no other power,
no other light.

The Quiet Watching

Have you seen the beginning of any world
from nothing,
what flies out of clouds, hatches on a branch,
not hanging on?
Or the tribe that climbed a stalk to enter here?
This is how much they all want
to be embodied in the grandeur of unfinished earth,
the first awkward entrance of being
having suddenly grown wings,
having turned over inside another,
undressing from their mothers,
or those breaking their way into the world,
eating the swaddling that held them,
or from the river swimming,
shining, without question. Red newts,
their eyes first open,
or the taller creatures standing
suddenly in the tall blowing grasses on plains
as if to say, Here we are in our naked finery,
our great birth,
our first clarity.

Winter Solstice

The first day of true winter.
The earth is already aslant with change.
I love the simplicity of chores.
of laying down
the grasses of summer,
the sound of horses eating,
frost on their manes,
breath visible in air,
the deep lung of their breath.

I rake frozen manure
and then I see it
on the mound I raked yesterday,
the snake skin, newly shed.

All night I wonder
how a snake left its earth den
from its companions woven together in a ball
and shed a skin so perfectly
in winter.

There is no answer
except perhaps a day's warm sun,
but in truth there will be no answer
unless from the split red tongue of that one

whose eyes never close,
who was awake
and now is back home
with its body curled into a three-foot secret
ten thousand years old.

Restless

I am always walking toward something,
somewhere. There is a coast
begging me to live at the edge,
a desert without the hardship of snow,
another country, another door.
I know there is a passage
the wind blows through,
the body breathes new,
and the road doesn't end,
as if one place dreams of another.
Even the earth wants to journey.
Today the sands of Mongolia
fill this sky with dust
from great distances,
the long glide of foreign atoms, different light.
Another dog lies at the door
breathing, feet moving as it sleeps.
Like me, always walking toward something,
even asleep, chasing, searching out
some treasure and then one day
we walk away from the body
leaving the skin clothes lying empty
and still travel on.

Turtle Watchers

Old mother at water's edge
used to bow down to them,
the turtles coming in from the sea,
their many eggs,
their eyes streaming water like tears,
and I'd see it all,
old mother as if in prayer,
the turtles called back to where they were born,
the hungry watchers standing at the edge of trees
hoping for food when darkness gathers.

Years later, swimming in murky waters
a sea turtle swam beside me
both of us watching as if clasped together
in the lineage of the same world
the sweep of the same current,
even rising for a breath of air at the same time
still watching.
My ancestors call them
the keepers of doors
and the shore a realm to other worlds,
both ways and
water moves the deep shift of life
back to birth and before
as if there is a path where beings truly meet,
as if I am rounding the human corners.

West

At night I feel the pull of the river west
as if all the land is a motion of slow time,
the atoms of water between the grains of soil,
also the rush of rain, all water, falling to travel back
to secret oceans, deep rivers, unseen waters.
Blood and tears, also, lonely and yearning
must rush toward the greater waters
and so where is the heart
in the early hour just before the bats leave?

Skin Boats

North, watching men stretch the hide,
the curve around wood,
the willow shoots for ribs
as if creating a body,
skin over wood
that might start to breathe,
that will pass through broken waters
away from searching ravens,
just like the ancestors
are there inside the curve of skin,
moving you, saying
may you know peace,
may you live in a world without weapons,
and remember, as you pass through
and across, wearing the skin of the animal
sitting with the tree, being the tree
that life flowed through
its bare roots for now not holding tight to earth,
remember the shore that surrounds a continent,
the history of life as it is spoken
along the edges, thresholds of all enchanted worlds,
the first ones say this,
pretending to be the breaking waves
and then you can set out, crying out
in all your full vigor.

The Creations of Water and Light

At night when the ocean is full
of its own created light, the luminescent eel,
the manta ray, the swimming-together
minions of the small. At night
when we are carried in the waters of this world
that existed before any of the gods
created earth-light or winged creatures,
I look through the relative darkness
and see the fire of plankton around your body
in the pure grace of shining light.

Fire and water are two elements
unlikely to join. Still, one sometimes comes of the other
as when the body creates its waters
from the fire of sexual yearning
and when the ocean reveals her light-bearing creatures
in the silken water that carries us.

At night when the ocean is teeming with the eggs
some creature has entrusted to the sea,
I remember how the body goes into itself,
at that moment between breaths
when it seems the tide of the body might pull away
before it comes back again. In the human body,
it is said, the gods of the ocean live below the navel

in the muscles that move like waves of their own accord
and when the bodies are pressed together,
skin against skin,
we can say we remember how ocean was formed,
we can say we knew it at the beginning of time,
the first element when something like gods
or makers fell into each other, cell by cell,
cell to cell,
and became something newly created,
boundless and light.

Affinity

Wild

This is not the horse. It is the poem,
even if it calls out for its sister,
even if it walks across the land
loving tall grasses and alfalfa
and is wild with its herd
speaking in ways the human mind
can't hear
so another part of the human
translates this animal in America,
the beloved partner of a woman
or man, knowing the herds of buffalo,
the loss of creation, the missing ones
who cannot be returned,
and so it longs to be this
translation
of life in the first light of morning
in the tall grasses of the prairie,
the hilltops from which it sees
there is no freedom here, not any more
in the mustang's changed history,
in the language that asks, What do you know
about this world, do you remember
the forgotten language wild,
can you still call it?

Walking

Walking on the road one night
my granddaughter says,
Grandma, are you afraid?
And I say, no, knowing this place
where the white dog lives,
where the chickens and birds hide eggs,
where the neighbor's geese go at night
leaving the river of new darkness.

And I know the worms
come up from the ground at night
so thick and beautiful you can hear them.
They shine and explore the black loam
and raise themselves to the night.
I have seen this.

I know fear has come down to us
from the first universe
where the beginnings of stars are never tame.

When she was born I was first to see her.
I held her up to be seen alive by ancestors
And beautiful spirits.

But I don't know what else is there.
If I think about it
if she cries at night,
I will join her.

Moving the Woodpile

Never am I careless,
yet when I lift the wood,
before I even see the wasp nest
I see spiders and ants, some preserved in pitch
and when I lift the wood
the bark falls from the log
and there are the silk cocoons,
worm-carved lines worked into the
woodflesh,
the beautiful work of insects
before they were white-winged, dusted creatures
who never asked the tree, What am I, who could I be,
never did they say, Oh world I love you
yet I loosen your skin and then I fly into the night.

As I lifted the log,
there they were in the wood, not yet anything,
the paper wasp nest of the barely alive,
only pale fingers searching, without eyes.

It's been so many years ago now
and still I have the haunting
memory and feel, standing there with the nest,
offering the wasps back their young,
but they could not approach a human holding their nest.

Maybe our sin is not enough
of us get on our knees and ever see
how everything small and nearly gone
is precious, the paper wasp nest,
made by the moment-by-moment creation of care.

Maybe our human sin is for us never to say
all these are great.
And I, the one who took it, in innocence, apart
as if being human I could not help it,
despite myself, generous and thieving
at one and the same time.

I've always wished
to hold the truly stolen, broken world together
but my every move is to break
by degrees, acres, even the smallest atom.

Still, from this other body continent
I offered them their young
and they could not come near the untamed woman,
only fly with desperation
and I think of this still
every evening, like a prayer,
that day holding out the nest for them, placing it down,
but never for them to approach,
and how I waited, how I watched.

Affinity: Mustang

Tonight after the sounds of day
have given way
she stands beneath the moon,
a gray rock shining.
She matches the land,
belonging.

She has a dark calm face,
her hooves like black stone
belong to the earth
the way it used to be,
long grasses
as grass followed rain
or wind laid down the plains of fall
or in winter now when
her fur changes and becomes snow
or her belly hair turns the color of red water willows
at the creek,
her legs black as trees.

These horses
almost a shadow,
broken.

When we walk together
in the tall grasses, I feel her
as if I am walking with mystery,
with beauty and fierce powers,
as if for a while we are the same animal
and remember each other from before.

Or sometimes I sit on earth
and watch the wind blow her mane and tail
and the waves of dry grasses
all one way
and it calls to mind
how I've come such a long way
through time
to find her.

Some days I sing to her
remembering the Kiowa man
who sang to cover the screams
of their ponies killed by the Americans,
songs I know in my sleep.

Some nights, hearing her outside,
I think she is to the earth
what I am to her,
belonging.

Last night it was her infant that died
after the kinship and movement
of so many months.
Tonight I sit on straw
and watch milk stream from her nipples
to the ground. I clean her face.
I've come such a long way through time
to find her and
it is the first time
I have ever seen a horse cry.

Sing then, the wind says,
Sing.

Emergence

I trust what all they say
that a world was made by songs, dreams,
and in our own world, the spin of another day,
that a woman god emerged from a lotus flower
and a man god was created in the image of a human,
that light was created by worlds
and all was formless void
before there was land
and the shining woman came up from ocean
out of the mists
or was made of the rib of a man
or that a clamshell opened
with a woman standing full-born,
and she gave sun to wheat.

First ocean, dark root.
We know, in some, there were betrayals,
a woman giving birth
in a place of animals,
the child falling into life
among the lowing cattle.
What grace,
born among the animals.
I think of a whale emerging tail-first
from its mother,

a foal, its clear hooves swimming into the world,
and that a mortal child
first opens to the world with a blue eye
that will darken in time.

Deer Dance

This morning
when the chill that rises up from the ground is warmed,
the snow is melted
where the small deer slept.
See how the bodies leave their mark.
The snow reveals their paths on the hillsides,
the white overcrossing pathways into the upper meadows
where water comes forth and streams begin.
With a new snow the unseen becomes seen.
Rivers begin this way.

At the deer dance last year,
after the clashing forces of human good and evil,
the men dressed in black,
the human women mourning for what was gone,
the evergreen sprigs carried in a circle
to show the return of spring.
That night, after everything human was resolved,
a young man, the chosen, became the deer.
In the white skin of its ancestors,
wearing the head of the deer
above the human head
with flowers in his antlers, he danced,
beautiful and tireless,

until he was more than human,
until he, too, was deer.

Of all those who were transformed into animals,
the travelers Circe turned into pigs,
the woman who became the bear,
the girl who always remained the child of wolves,
none of them wanted to go back
to being human. And I would do it, too, leave off being human
and become what it was that slept outside my door last night.

One evening I hid in the brush south of here
and watched at the place where they shed their antlers
and where the deer danced, it was true,
as my old grandmother said,
water came up from the ground
and I could hear them breathing at the crooked river.
The road there I know. I live here,
and always when I walk it
they are not quite sure of me,
looking back now and then to see that I am still
far enough away, their gray-brown bodies,
the scars of fences,
the fur never quite straight,
as if they'd just stepped into it.

Dimensions

How is it decided
who among us has hands,
gill slits, who will gather up
a small thing
waiting too far from the ocean
to be alive or return
with the kelp and its bulbs of gold,
and the creature we see almost through,
see in the light of morning
among the many baleful closures of the ocean.

How is it decided
who will gather up the small thing
seeming lifeless
and return it to water as its grave
only to watch it slowly open;
jellyfish like a pulse,
a robe of orange splendor
in the finery of ocean creation.

I see the wave, with a curve of light,
the force of it, one after another,
not wondering if it is the ocean.
I see the infinite pastures of water,

some with the newly born, some
with the just as newly gone.

Here is a place of sliding worlds,
at the birthplace of Chief Seattle
whose people he said would always be
among those with bodies.
And how is it decided who has dominion
of the flesh
to pass through unseen
or on its way to being spirit,
forgetting the brief distances in time.

I don't know who lives here,
if they are happy
in that slide of cells
that created and birthed them
or who is it that decided who has hands,
who can speak,
who is light?

Children of Light

See her. I do.
Kneel to her. I do.
What sweetness she is.
Coax her, as if you can make her believe
she will live in a shining meadow
or a cave of crystal, as if the first step
is toward an opening of sun
or star-filled night.
She will open,
from my first self
and lighten her being
with a brightness of step
and I see her like I am
myself, love her, hold her,
a hand at the back of the neck
and the girl child in my center
born to a world
not in prison, not killed as an infant,
the best of fortune
not in a flooding delta,
a war, not with a machete
to the neck, lucky enough,
not with her own child
killed before her.
She is the carried gift,

how very tender
like the turning silver
of the fish in the pond at night,
beautiful, exhausted
to come passing into the circle of the world.
She is the grain-filled, grape-filled,
milk-filled, light.
She has no fur,
no thick hide.
No wonder we are warriors.
Come on child,
even if you will never understand,
even if you will be angry
with your own kind.

The Night Constant

At night, outside the house,
I feel the lion
near the black pine trees.
Sometimes walking on the road
before the eyeshine in darkness
I can tell it is
walking just before me,
cutting across the field
toward the dog and goat.
I feel it with the naked eye of skin,
the fine hair, the animal trappings of my body
begin to rise, a beast remaining,
and there is a feeling, too, of awe and respect,
and, yes, remorse
for our kind who have tried to reach heaven,
learn a universe
and found stars that swallow light,
that bounded darkness is a matter
between light and broken light,
and we don't even know
the animals that walk outside our sleep
yet we have traveled there so often
there are not so many of them now
where light falls across the hunting grounds
we call a world that's small

because we've matched it to ourselves
and with all the lies we tell ourselves
so we won't see the world collapse
but when it does
it is not from what is known
but from what is never seen.

Secret

It is still dark out in the garden.
From out of the moist ground
some things bloom only at night,
the moonflower, primrose, the nightshade,

and it was dark
in the garden from which we grew
and woke.

How far light must travel toward us
without that one going to the river at night
holding the water falling from the bowl, her hands,
to say *this is light*

This, so far, is the smallest journey, when you think of stars.

All I really know is every night
the wind returns here
but I never know where it's been
and it moves the leaves of the open moonflower.

Light is one thing not prisoner to gravity.
So it is with darkness.
And the shadows may be in us,
but we should live by what we feel.
There's darkness. And somewhere is the remembered,
the record, the great humanity of being.

The Thief of Light

Without a map,
without a country,
the man stole it
and no plants grew.
Nothing rose up,
no sight of faces loved,
everything known by feel and memory
only, by sound or the touch
of a hand, the placement of a foot,
being how it was navigated.
There was finally the feel
of a world, the feel
of a forgotten footstep,
a remembered boundary of skin
knowing the way
as sharks know in water,
the paths of ancestors,
and the great turtles across land
travel as if all was safe,
and a touch in the street
may be a hand of kindness,
a hand with dreams.

Fox

Every day he announces his presence, clockwork.
I see the fox, the tail so full
and I want to touch it.
The face so sweet, the white muzzle,
the way it moves from one side of the hill to another,
memorizing every stone,
the way it lies down on ground to watch me,
as if it is easy and not just fear, not hunger.
And when I see it
I have to love and hate it
because its body is my cat,
my neighbor's cat,
and even though I hurt
I know that this was not a gunshot,
not an accident on the road,
not a long illness.
This is god swallowing what it must.

Escape

It is sometimes to stand still
or pretend to be larger than another,
or to be hidden in a stand of forest,
a dark bed of kelp. Soon you will be
opening eyes to watch for the lean,
when they come toward you,
or the destroyers that open a world
of disappearance.
Nightless. Sleepless.
The moon on the sage growing
silver in the light, rain in the leaves.
You feel the plants if you are quiet enough.
Here quickness has no use.

Yet the fish sees all ways and swims away.
The eel has escaped the teeth of the larger.
One frog changes color to match a poison one,
or an insect looks like a leaf,
and blessed is the lizard that loses a tail
that will grow back. How simple,
how divine the pardon, the plan
that grants it more chances than the rest.

And we who walk upright
think we have escaped, as divine

as losing a tail. But what it is
we don't know. How we stand
at the gracious threshold between
the animal and the heartless
or loving,
before the spirit escapes the body.

And before then, if you are lucky,
you will sleep out in the dry grasses one day
and wake to see the five wild turkeys
for only a second
before they disappear from sight
so mysteriously, so quickly, as they do.

From Far Away

Today the sky is misted
from sandstorms in far Mongolia,
as the day when the red dust rose
in Monument Valley, a place where the wind is holy.

Life, it looks like sunrise
or the slow approach of clouds,
all on their way to the unknown.

Or, as with a storm, I have to wonder
if thunder travels along its edge
above the place of green frogs in red clay.
You can almost hear them
at dusk when the past begins.

The Hidden

There are the far universes, the undiscovered
ocean depths, the hidden magma,
as if every morning you've been forsaken
and given smallness which you must accept as truth.

And some earthly paradise,
how reverent and radiant
the first fronds of green beginnings,
the shine of moonlight behind a cloud,
or the pearl in an ordinary shell.

There are the often-described blue sheep
of the Himalayas,
the grain of gold beneath the earth.

Oh traveler, what if the far river had not been created.
Where then would you dream of going?
What if you hadn't believed the story
or trusted directions through the desert
all those dry miles?

I don't care what you call it,
the human other portion, trust, belief.
What if you looked at it all aslant?
Then you would never have arrived

in the good red land, the heat,
suddenly finding the spring
and the wild horses.

Paradise has always been just out of sight.

Shine

Sometimes, after the rain
I see their trails in mud,
the shining earthworms who made
their way upward, eyeless from the roots.
And there are the backs of dung beetles
shining, the yellow slugs moist
near the leaves.

And then, by day,
the satin blue backs of flies,
lovely, veined and transparent wings
as if the signature of creation
is written on the small,
the unloved
and they are measured
equal to the large,
matched by their unpraised light.

Then there is the cosmos
created by spiders.
Do not slight them
who at birth
spin their hundred strands of silk
from their own bodies,

and then you've seen it, the drop of dew
in their round silk, woven.

The night, too, is a place of marvels,
the creature light,
the eyes of the skunk and rats,
not vermin, but all the beginning of the great,
dark to the mind, light to the heart.

At the Water

What if you are in a place fire can't burn?
Fish, that's your home.
Knives can't cut water
and no one has fists.
I see the amber rooms underneath
Where light meets green
and nymphs of mayflies hide beneath jeweled shells
as if the gold of sun is not enough.
Among the old leaves you hide,
sliver of fish, like a small moon alone
where the currents move you
slightly, veils of fins waving.
Fish, don't you hear the river calling you?
You live in a place knives don't cut.
Fish, with the eye that never closes,
I want to follow you
To the wide, wide waters.

Hearts

Looking through sound at my grandson
before he is born, the spine in the darkness,
the small white heart beating. Then
I saw them lift him to the world. Oh,
he has loved our horses, been my green branch.
Now he knows anger,
thicket, fire.

When I was a girl I sat on the rung of a ladder
and asked my father if he killed anyone during the war.
I remember the birds were singing and how
he, that gentle man, changed to anger, narrowing
eyes: Never ask that question again.

Oh the astonishing shadows
of men and women
in the light of a simple question.

When I saw the war, the burning children,
I wanted to hurt the killers. It is the way one metal
in the presence of a magnet becomes magnetic.

The god took away something from some of us
and the heart is the first thing to go.
Some days I think of that small unborn heart

plucked from the stem of infancy.
Some days I want to give myself
to no part of humanity, fallen from the ladder
so old now it has lost its rungs,
just two sticks of wood trying to walk

Wind Circle

In the place of worn earth
we walk on its softness
to the red canyon wall
with its people waiting, speaking centuries
in a place where all time is first time
even those older, carved.

Walking, the tailprints of lizard,
the layers where water passed through
its own roundness, the globe mallow blooming
an orange desert
in the red morning light, we red women
smile at the lines and feet of lizards in sand,
their lives written here, the mice, too,
and then around the plants
where wind has passed through mountains
and the stone people stand
in the perfect circle it has blown them
like a whirlwind, a dance worn into sand
perfectly round
a compass reading
here, now, then.

And in the time of fear
when the enemy came
there was this one plant that kept people alive.

There is that almost constant
from the universe, the sun, from
the mystery of where wind comes,
writing its circle with the brush of a plant.

Sweet smell
the dust,
the wall, the ladders carved to sky,
the people and the animals on rock,
the man and woman flute players
and the sky overhead with the woman, the man,
the snake the eagle, a circle
called Wind.

Reveal

Dark matter where the space
between stars,
the space between bodies, is not there. Still
there is the journey home
to a house in the trees, the body
sheltered by forests, the fallen, the upgrown,
the rise of mineral earth, the traveling fluids,
the leaves each with their own green lantern light
veined, breathing human air
and you walk to this house from darkness unprepared
from the first breath
that opens you to the world
with eyes that do not see what you are made of
as if a human is a plant that opens only at night,
trusting, even asleep
in the pathway of blood
the organs that could cover miles
uncontained,
as if space is inside the human.
Time, too, the uncounted minutes,
not those that began with the birth of Christ
or even with the quickening,
but the older revelations
inside the human the secrets
that one day will be known

as when the storm took away the sand of the beach
leaving black lava underneath,
or when the mudslide revealed a forgotten village
or when the water diviner found a lost city
covered with ash.

This is what you are
and will be, divined, found.
Something underneath,
the inward minutes,
larger than the body they live inside.

Or maybe it is more than that
as when the light drops into the ocean
when night begins.

Or less, if you could call it that,
like the robin egg that fell to the ground.
Less, too, than was imagined,
the human salvaged
from the lives and deaths of other worlds
so small in the galaxy of immortal beings,
passions so seemingly large,
accidental atoms of stars and dust.

And more. There is to a person a mystery,
the inward map, the sixth sense,
and then there is the remembering

the parts unknown and the knowledge
of science that says
there is no true sight of the world.
The eye, remember, with its straight
dark channels of vision, turns the world over,
not that it rights it.

And then there is the outside world,
not just vision, bright or dark,
but bone hunters searching the great forgotten distance
of the past, prophets seeing the future,
gazing into night sky,
entrails, crystals, or fire,
and it doesn't matter when they look at the sky
through a piece of glass
and infinity is how far you can see
through something solid,
but there is an angle of sight
that fits or reads the present bone

in the way there is not a
change of time, except measured
and told in words directly revealed
from before instruments and the lens.

And then, when you reach the forest body
with its lantern light
you find the branches covered with snow

and walk to it
and now knowing
the breath that goes out
may become something unbound and clear.

Now it is now, the winter count begins,
the hides with the old ones painted with stories
that show what has occurred,
these stories, too, divinely lived and told
without instruments or lenses
to enlarge a sight.
Open it, the animal skin, the flesh, the primal hide,
and read the names and deeds, those of a history
that made this time
desperately unremembered
and suddenly known.

Call

I don't know what you call it
when the lion sounds wounded and calls
the smaller animals
with their healthy coats and paws,
and they go as if death knows their language
and can change it to another.
The wolf, too, knows the words of elk and moose
and how to call them forward
and with the coyote the lovely vole arises
with soft fur from underground.
This, this is how some hear their god
and wander off toward it or him
and then are taken in
while the god walks on mighty and full,
passing others, generous at last.